REALTOR UNMASKED

Rookie 2 Top Dog

Mistakes Realtors Make from day 1

STOP NOW

The Clock Is Ticking

Written and Designed by

Sue Edman Beckenham ©

MY WONDERFUL FAMILY

To my beautiful boys, who hated those dreaded phone calls. When I started my career, it was just the 3 of us.

We didn't meet their stepdad until some years later. The boys were very proud of their mum even though it drove them nuts.

The all, watched as I too jumped from office to office in search of that niche, we are all in search of.

How they have given me the love and patience in those hard times when arriving home in tears, rejections or deep disappointments have sent me plummeting into depression... temporarily of course, we salespeople have the ability to bounce back quickly.

When at times when we as a family gathered for special occasions, when mums phone would be ringing off the hook, on Christmas Day or just as a movie started.

My partner was patient and understanding, being from a sales background himself, he knew the dedication it took to become successful. Without that person in your life, your bouncing board, confidant, shoulder to cry on, your journey will be tough.

Thank you from the bottom of my heart. Gary, Dion, Trent and Ma.

TO YOU, FELLOW AGENTS

Dedicated to all those hard working real estate agents/consultants/property managers that have worked relentlessly and tirelessly in a Property industry that is forever unforgiving, competitive and ruthless in all its glory, arrogance and yet, when it gets in your blood as it did mine, it will offer you some friendships from wonderful people from all walks of life, some of the best agents are not the richest of agents by way of income, but they are rich in integrity and in the respect you will encounter from the most humble to the most opulent in this Professional arena.

Good people who only want to earn a living, strive to maintain their own personal integrity and honesty, are up against others who lack such qualities and do all they can to undermine you, rip you off and leave without a thought of the damage they have done.

Watch your backs...

MY MOTTO IS NOW YOURS

"If you can't …

Eat…. Sleep… Breath

Real Estate,

……..then, you shouldn't

be in it".

TABLE OF CONTENTS

INTRODUCTION TO REAL ESTATE

ATTENTION NEWBIES – beware

After 20+ years as a real estate sales agent, having owned and run my own real estate business, been employed by several Principals, worked in a cross section of areas and calibre of properties from the low end of the market to the high end. My journey is not yet cover.

Having sold over a thousand properties, worked alongside of hundreds of colleagues, I now feel I am in a position to assist other agents who are either about to enter the property industry or even and particularly those who have been in the industry for a long time but never seem to find that right office.

I know what it's like being a new Sales agent to the property market. It's like being thrown into the lion's cage at dinner time. You are probably sitting there thinking that has to be an over exaggerated description of entering the industry for the first time!

NO EXAGERATION

THE BIGGER THE DOLLAR – THE BIGGER THE SHARK

I can assure you I am not exaggerating.

It is also the most competitive, glamorous, and one of the highest paid commissions in any industry, and with it comes its demons.

THE KNIVES WILL BE OUT

When you think of how much a single sales commission can be, you can understand how much your colleagues or your other offices in town wanted that listing too. They also may have appraised the property, but they lucked out, and you got the listing.

$10,000 - $20,000 - $30,000 or more, has now gone into your bank account at settlement. Certainly, the knives are going to be out. We are all chasing that Listing. It's unfortunately human nature.

GET OUT NOW

YOU'RE GOING TO BE CHEWED UP AND SPAT OUT

If you think now that people don't act like that, and you still use the idea that if you treat people the right way and be nice, everything will be ok, then get out now. You are going to be chewed up and spat out.

This industry is not for you.

3

AN EVOLVING INDUSTRY

How I started

The Real Estate Industry as far as salespeople, principals, offices, procedures, materials used, and commissions are concerned have certainly changed immensely in many ways over the years.

When I first joined in 1993, I had come from Retail. I was very good at selling SHOES, FASHION and COSMETICS.

Yes, that's right, I had absolutely no experience in selling property, much less know anything about the market I was about to enter, interest rates, nor the area in which I had chosen.

I had always bought House and Garden magazines, and gone to open homes, display villages etc, to see different styles of decorating and one day thought how nice it would be to become a Sales Agent because I could spend all day looking in beautiful homes. And believe it or not, newbies are still thinking along these lines even today, they join the industry because of that very same reason. So 'some' things haven't changed.

As it turned out, the market was depressed, interest rates were 18% and still rising, agents were leaving in droves to go do 'paid jobs' or return to previous industries that paid wages. Some were even working at a paying job part time and doing real estate in their spare time.

There were no buyers, and every suburb had hundreds of homes on the market waiting for that illusive buyer. They had missed the 'Boom' and when they realised interest rates were rising and there would be no buyers, they quickly placed their homes on the market in the hope to beat the hike. And there they stayed.

Why wasn't I told?

You may think I was dumb. But if you have experienced raising a family on your own, with no family or friends around at all to advise you otherwise, dreaming of getting out of the rut and the struggle of life in general, you will understand.

And here I was, a single mum, green as the tree in your front garden, no experience and thought 'better'. Yes, I was going to set the world on fire. My little boys would be provided with wonderful toys, excursions, and private schools, they were never to go without again. (I thought) As a single mum, I had big dreams too.

OFFICES I HAVE WORKED IN

MY FIRST OFFICE

My first office I chose because a friend had suggested I call him, apparently, he had a good reputation of being an honest man who had respect for his agents. And was a non-selling principal.

At my interview, he actually warned me of the property slump and suggested I stay in Retail and do real estate on weekends. I decided to ignore his suggestion and said that I would go hammer and tong to make him proud.

He saw I was keen and offered me a retainer knowing I was a single mother. This was to be paid in cash and when I started to make sales, I would pay him back.

Clearly, he had confidence in what I wanted to do and was going to support me. So, I resigned at my retail position, another surprise was in store for me there though.

BEWARE OF WELL-MEANING FRIENDS

I went to my store manager to tell him I was resigning, and he tried very hard to talk me out of it. He said I was a valued member of their team and he had high hopes for me. (even though I was recently knocked back for a promotion because the Floor Manager hated me) and all applications had to go through her. I knew I had no hope there of advancement.

So, I held my head high, said thank you but I am joining real estate. I will never forget the look on his face.

Later I knew what it meant. I feel he was thinking I was a very silly girl., that the property market was in a bad state.

So off I went. My first week I got to know the office procedures, rules, pecking order, and went to my first sales meeting which was scary. Everyone know what they were talking about and I knew nothing. All I knew is that I passed my course with flying colours, high distinction, I looked great, and obtained my Real Estate license which I framed and proudly hung it on the wall above my desk.

I had flyers printed out by the office girl and off I went letterbox dropping. Day after day, week after week. The principal as he'd promised, left my weekly retainer in my In Tray in an envelope.

It was an office of 5 salespeople and a big team of property management for their rental properties. I was the only female in the sales team.

MY LAST DAY AT MY FIRST OFFICE

It was in the middle of summer, and I had been out all- day letterbox dropping and door knocking to get my first listing. I walked in hot and sweaty and slumped down at my desk. There was the usual yellow envelope with company logo on the front in my tray and immediately I noticed it had been opened.

A salesman approached me, and it was clear that if he hadn't opened it, he certainly knew what the contents were! I asked who had opened this. His reply was 'whose leaving you money, what's it for?'

One of the office girls came to my defence telling him that it's my 'Retainer'. Well, in those days you just didn't get a retainer. Then came the snide remarks and one of them said that 'Nobody gets retainers unless they're sleeping with the boss'. The guys all laughed but I knew that's what they really thought. So, I left the envelope with the office girl, cleaned out my desk and left. Never to return.

In hindsight, I should have stuck it out. And I'll tell you why later in this book.

KEYWORDS: Non-Selling Principal

OFFICE FROM HELL

After a short break from the industry, the property market had started to pick up and I'd decided it time to give it another try. I answered an advertisement in the jobs column in the newspaper and got the job. The lady was just so lovely, it was her own business and I just adored her. (at first). I did learn a lot from her, she kind of took me under her wing. It was a tiny office; they didn't have a secretary or receptionist. When she wasn't there, she put her husband who was out of work at the front desk. He too was very nice. It was a family business, Principal, her husband, myself and another salesman who had become my friend. He too was relatively new to the industry.

It didn't take us long to realise that I was being conned. She would advertise a property in the Saturday paper, send me off to the Open times that she had advertised, have the office phone number in the advertisement (nobody had mobiles or computers in those days) While I (and the other salesman also) were at the open for inspections, the husband would be taking the enquiries, sending the buyers to the address and then passing the leads onto his wife the Principal. SOLD. She would tell us that another agency sold it. At first, we believed her because she was SOOO nice. Until one day, I had had enough and resigned and walked out.

That night I called the other salesman, told him I had resigned...." So, have I" he chirped into the phone. And for the same reasons.

KEYWORD: <u>SELLING</u> Principal

SUCCESS AT LAST

You Think???

As a competent and successful sales agent, you are being observed constantly by other agencies, in particular other Principals. You are going to get "Headhunted" regularly. It's great for the ego believe me.

It is hard not to be flattered to a point that when they say that you are that good that they want you to join their team. Wow, suddenly you have reached

'Success' you are now a successful real estate sales agent that has earned a reputation by the number of Sold signs around the area. Can you imagine the size of my EGO? Yep, it was pretty big.... enormous in fact.

Hahah......

BANG......

It didn't, once again, take me long to realise that there was not just one Selling Principal, but there were 2!!!!!!

Will I ever get this RIGHT I thought to myself?!!!!

The Receptionist was to put ALL enquiries through to the Principal on duty at the time. So, you can only imagine who the leads were going to go to right? Do you honestly think that when a seller calls the office to list his or her property, that with a selling principal it's not going to go to him first? She is being paid by your fellow sales colleague, where do you think that multimillion-dollar listing is going to go to? The one on roster? No way! It will go quietly and directly to the Principal. 100% of the commission goes to him/her.

DON'T BE NAÏVE....

Both principals were doing very well indeed thank you very much, but their sales agents were struggling. But guess what? Talk about gullible. I worked in 2 offices with 2 principals. But I will fill you in soon the reasons why that happened.

KEYWORD: <u>Selling</u> Principals x 2

THE COST OF RUNNING A REAL ESTATE OFFICE IS ASTRONOMICAL

Your Principal too has worked hard.

Here are some of the major expenses.

Sales offices have huge overheads every month.

- Indemnity Insurance
- Company Car Insurance, Services, and Registration
- Rental of the premises
- Electricity
- Phone Lines
- Stationary – Printer Ink & Maintenance – Paper & much more
- Advertising in Newspapers & Multimedia, Letterbox drops
- Monthly subscriptions on Internet property platforms like realestate.com – Domain,

Facebook, and other platforms around the world. Each property uploaded for sale or for rent must be paid for and usually first by the office.

- Book-keeping, Accountants and Auditors. All have high fees. Real estate Directors have 'end of month' and this is done by either a well paid office Manager, or Accountant, they have obligations to their Offices of Fair Trading to get an Audit on their books about 3 times a year which can go into the thousands, depending on the size of the business, sales and rental properties, not to mention "Spot Audits" once a year, and accountant charges once again at the end of the financial year for their services.

- Staff Wages. Depending on the size of the Rent Roll (Rental Properties managed) as well as some salespeople who may be on Retainers, Cleaners & Maintenance.

- Software premiums. For example, book-keeping programs charge monthly premiums. Software to upload and market properties have monthly premiums.

So, as you can see, on a monthly basis, office overheads are enormous. Do you blame the owner to want to be able to list and sell as well? They have to feed their families as well, they have to pay their mortgages, put their kids through school, be seen to be successful so drive the latest vehicle, have a lovely home, it all costs money.

They have also been in your shoes before, they too have been a rooky, worked their way into top salesperson, perhaps bought the office from the previous owner, all along they have sold property to be able to one day own their own real estate office. Sales are in their blood, and their bank managers are also out for their blood. Of course, they will be wanting to Sell too. In many cases, it won't be against you? But in most cases, it will.

KEYWORD: <u>Selling</u> Principals

MISS MATCH

This one will confuse you somewhat.

I applied for a job which I thought was advertised by the actual Principal but when I rocked up at a City interview in a high-rise building, I quickly realised that this was not the real estate office, it was an employment agency working on behalf of an agency finding them staff.

I was sent to an interview with the said Principal, sat with him for an hour asking what I thought were all the right questions. He said that he had to discuss my application with another party, and we parted ways. Before I got my car out onto the highway the phone rang, it was him offering me a position. I was thrilled because he was such a great guy, very down to earth, great sense of humour and I had a good feel about it.

It was a big sales team, but I had worked my way to 'Top Dog' (typical name in the industry) earning an incredible wage. By this time, I had learned how to

'Watch my back'. As glamourous as it may seem being a Real Estate agent to outsiders, on the inside, it can be treacherous. I found out that one of the agents would sneak back into the office at night, get into the boss's files, and got all our passwords and codes so that he could see exactly what we were doing, who our clients were, upcoming leads .... the lot. There was another agent who would stay until after other agents left the office making out that she was working, but although she didn't have the 'nouse' to do what he did, she still rummaged through sales agents draws and diaries. I found this out one morning I came in and my diary was missing. I searched everywhere, went home thinking I had left it there, but in the end, I found it on her desk. The following week, she had listed 2 properties that were my leads.

Apart from that, I was happy there, the boss didn't sell, he just oversaw the Rental team and met us up on Sales meetings etc.

2 OFFICES MERGE

Yes, he was a great boss then. However, as times started to change, leads and sales started to dry up, the 2nd office he also owned seemed the obvious choice to move his team to saving on overheads etc. The other office also had a Principal (my boss's partner) so once again it looked like I was to be going into a premise with 2 Principals. Ok I thought, that's cool, I will keep doing what I do and move across too.

But the other office had a Selling Principal and now my boss decided to start to sell too. It became dog eat dog. Leads were fought over, the market was sliding, receptionists forwarded leads to the boss's never to be seen again until a contract went down. So, my lovely boss had turned into yet another Selling Principal of which I had become very disillusioned by. It was time to jump ship. And jump ship I did.

KEYWORD: Non-Selling TO Selling Principal

MY BEST OFFICE EVER

With a Non-Selling Christian Principal

I had been told about a non-selling principal in a lower priced area which I knew nothing about, it had underground mining in some of its suburbs and not just Black Soil but Reactive Black Soil. The story was that he was a lovely man and knew more about the area than anyone.

I called him and had an interview. The first question he asked me "What church do you go to?" although I am a believer, I had no time for church raising kids on my own. So, I made one up. He was happy and employed me straight away ha-ha.

If you are a newbie and stumble into an office like this one, you have it made. Do not move from it. Ever!!!

He paid a retainer, small to start with. Then raised it as you proved yourself that you had potential. The commission structure was fair, and believe me, when I tell you an average commission in that area today is between $15,000 to $20,000 before it's broken up Office/Salesperson but at that time the average commission was between $1,500 and $3,000 (Halve that as your take home commission.)

Yet with that, again, I worked myself up to top dog bringing home over $100,000 so you can only imagine how fast we were selling property? That was early 2000's, some homes doubled over a few months as a Boom was looming.

KEYWORD: Non-Selling Principal

YOU WILL BE CHEWED UP AND SPAT OUT

Colleagues and Other Agency Staff

Oh....and some Selling Principals.

This is a wonderful industry. It offers flexibility, social life, you will get to meet people from all walks of life, and the money can be fantastic, depending on your commission breakup and the present climate in the real estate industry and global economy.

Try not to go out in the good times, buying brand new cars, a world trip, buying a larger property, in other words don't over commit yourself because the industry can come to a grinding halt overnight. For instance, if Wall Street crashes, there's a global pandemic, global financial crisis all of which have happened in the last 10 years from writing this book. Banks stop lending unless it's to a first home buyer or the buyer has loads of capital in a present home.

Sales are only happening because the governments have offered First Home Buyers Grants. This is great for 1st home buyers and he is building industry but not so much for the homeowner that is wanting to upgrade or sell out and go back to renting.

Then your spending days will also come to a grinding halt, that new car you love you will grow to hate because it has blown your budgeting to shreds.

It's always easy to tell when the property market slides and sales are not happening, you just have to go for a drive around the car yards and see how they are bulging at the seams with more BMW's and SUV's that were owned by real estate agents. Ask any used car salesman about his/her thoughts on this. You will also see in your suburb's lovely cars on sides of roads with For Sale signs on them. If you take the time to google the mobile number on the handwritten sign…. you will find it is owned by a real estate agent.

Just Say'n…. lol……

Getting back to your colleagues and principals. Because the commissions are so high, unless the office has very strict listing and selling strategies, rules in place, then you are going to have to watch your back.

There are some very aggressively strong agents in some offices, who will walk over you to get your listing, or I should say STEAL your listing.

Some agents are only there to pay the bills, they don't want to set the world on fire with Awards and extremely high incomes. They've been in the industry too long to be like that and will more often than not want to help you and take pride in your success's.

KEEP RECORDS

But they are not all nice. And I can't say this enough. Keep records on EVERYTHING. **DIARISE EVERYTHING.** EVERY CONVERSATION. EVERY MEETING. And above all be HONEST. White lies are LIES and can find yourself in court.

OTHER AGENCY STAFF

At some stage in your first few months, you may have a property that another Sales Agent at your opposition agency has a buyer for. When I say that you can be Chewed up and Spat Out, I meant also from another agency salespeople.

Example:

I had an exclusive listing. A local investor phoned me to arrange for a viewing. When I turned up, the owner was outside and an agent from another agency was inside with MY buyer, the one who had phoned for a viewing. Clearly, she had also been dealing with him but didn't have any properties he liked so piggy backed on mine.

I phoned my then principal, and she then phoned hers. Both Principals arrived, arguing out in the street who was in the right and who was in the wrong.

The buyer was disgusted and left the property. He said he had been misled by the other agent; she had told him she had the listing too.

The gutless principals both backed down, and nothing was done about it.

Who suffered? The poor old lady trying to sell her property. She didn't ask for this to happen.

So never underestimate your opposition. And that can be within your own office or another office.

Particularly when stock is low in all the offices, and homeowners are getting all the agencies to appraise their homes. When you are the winner in obtaining the listing, the knives will be out both in your own office and out in the field. Ideally it would be perfect if a colleague has a buyer, and you don't. Fabulous.

Always follow your State's fair-trading rules and real estate regulations. If you do that, whatever another agent says about you will go no further. Keep records ALWAYS.

Don't get too friendly with other agents.

Over a glass of wine and a few laughs you may spill something confidential. Don't risk it. Loose lips sink ships.

Success comes in different forms

You can only find the right office if you ask the right questions in the beginning at your interview. Once the right answers are given, it is then up to you how successful you will become. Don't forget that success comes in many different forms. Are you are aiming for the success of a top rating agent with a high income? Is money not what drives you, but obtaining the respect of family, friends and the community? Or are you just wanting to maintain a modern car for yourself and your partner, own a middle-class home and be able to pay the bills at the end of the month?

INTERVIEWS

Interviews can be nerve wracking; we can never get out the questions in the heat of the moment for many reasons.

Often the interviewer is from a recruitment agency and all they want is for you to send on your resume/CV, meet you briefly, forward their findings on to the Employer with their suggestions as to whether this person is worthy of hiring or not. Suddenly you get a call from the agency asking when you can start and your off and running. or should I say on a downhill slide of …. Failing.

Alternatively, you are interviewed by an employer who is either in a hurry and makes it clear as you sit down that he has an appointment to get to, gives you a quick rundown of just how successful the other sales agents are doing and how high a profile they have in their chosen area…… or the absolute opposite side of the coin…… when they just want to talk about themselves then ask you when you can start if you laugh at all their weird jokes and nod at everything they say. Still, you have not asked the right questions but starting Monday!

Then within days, weeks and sometimes it takes months before you realise you have wasted your time and that you are not going to make much, in fact working for a food chain would give you more money and respect for yourself.

JUMPING SHIP

So, you jump ship. It might take you months to find another position. Then the merry-go-round starts up all over again! Before you know it, 6 months have gone by and you have not earned a cent., bills are building up and debt collector calls have started coming in.

In this book, the Rookies will learn how not to waste years in a stale office with a lacking fairness to the salespeople. You will know the right questions to ask at your interview. These questions will be the make or break of a new career you are about to enter into. If you take note from an experienced agent that has made every mistake in the book in choosing an office time and time again.

The Experienced Sales Agent who has been in the industry a while, and done what I did, jumping from office to office... You too will now be able to find the right office at long last and reignite your career in real estate. You will be confident in the fact that you asked the right questions and the answers you got from your prospective employer ticked all the box's. The years pass us so fast; I would now be living in a mansion in Hope Island on the Gold Coast had I known all the boxes to tick 20+ years ago.

Here we go again

I class myself as an intelligent person, I am a good judge of character, and yet time and time again I made the same mistakes. I only wish someone else had put out a book like this to stop me from making these mistakes that stagnated my progress somewhat.

Stand strong, don't be fobbed off at your interview. Remember this…. it's YOU who are doing the interviewing!! If you remember this, you can't go wrong. After you have asked your questions, and received the answers, allow the small talk to filter through. Small talk is a must, don't dismiss as unimportant, this is how you will have an idea if your new employer has a sense of humour (much needed in this industry) or an annoying personality.

Enjoy this book, keep it with you. It is your bible when you are on the hunt for a new

DREAMING OF A BETTER LIFE?

– You can have it ALL! AT a COST......

Most people interested in selling, whether it be Shoes, Cosmetics or Cars, have at some stage wondered if what it would be like to sell real estate in some form or another. One of the most perceptually glamorous professions in our modern world. Highfliers. Go-getters. The beautiful people!

You may see your local agent rushing around in his/her flashy and shiny SUV, BMW or Mercedes, watched them with admiration as they 'strut their stuff' at an Open for Inspection or Auction and admired from afar, their obvious confidence and air of perhaps arrogance in some cases. You wonder if you too could stand up next to the Auctioneer and mingle with your buyers encouraging them to increase their bid, or hold an Open for Inspection, welcoming curious buyers who could very well put in an offer that very day. $$$ How exciting!

DRESS CODE

In most top end agencies, the dress code is very high. Men wear suits and ties, clean shaven, just the type of mum or dad would prefer you bring home. This attire is expected and no less is accepted by a certain element of the community. The ladies adorn expensive suits, immaculately groomed with the latest hair style, heels and manicures, carrying the latest brand handbag or brief- case, and not purchased on an international mock-up brand website, briefcase in one hand, on mobile phone in the other. How glamorous you think this job would be! Could this be you too?

Can you imagine the office you would love to work in? Modern, large desks, privacy so that you can talk without being overheard in your negotiations, air-conditioned of course, your big photo and profile blurb in the front window as "Salesperson of the Month"

......meet Jenny Jones.

How deliciously exciting!!! How proud you would be at your School Reunion when your high school archrival asks what you had done with yourself over the last few years?! .... Would you feel great to say how successful you had become? You could say that you are a

"Licensed Real Estate Agent"! (a no more admired or envied profession in the world.) What, with Social

Media and Reality shows about Millionaire Mansions being sold by go-getter sales agents., it all is so glamorous, or so it seems to the world outside the arena of the real estate agent.

AT WHAT COST

And yes, you can have all this, but it often comes at an enormous cost. Is it all it is cracked up to be? Will I walk in on my first day and be sitting in my own large modern office? Have a sale on the 2nd day? Money in the bank by the end of the week from my first commission? Trade my old Ford for a Mercedes? Wow, I will be rolling in money!

Stay reading!......

You are about to find out the reality of being a Real Estate Sales Consultant, Real Estate Sales Executive,

Property Agent, Property Manager.... whatever you want to call yourself, the nuts and bolts of what it's all about, and the 10 mistakes rookie real estate agents make, even agents who have been in the industry for many years, do not know what questions to ask at their next interview. At interviews we all get caught up in the moment, even though we take along a note pad, we seem to allow the interviewer to have full control of the half hour you may have with them. The 'small talk' may seem a waste of time, and it is unless you use it to your benefit. Don't walk out of the meeting feeling as if you had made a new friend but didn't get the job, or that you have just 'bared your soul' and still may not get the job, and probably won't because you have shown the interviewer more than required (too much information.?)

Confused yet? You should be!!! Stay tuned, I will show you what to say and what not to say. The strategic questions you should ask and answers your prospective employer should give.

This book is 'Gold'. No employer or colleague is going to give you this information I am about to share.

ROOKIES

If you are a Rookie, completed your studies and have your sales consultant certificate, obtained your Selling Agent's License and looking for your first job as a Real Estate Agent? you need to read, read, and read again this book.

Memorise my suggestions and you will find that perfect office that suits your needs. A career as a real estate sales agent is very exciting. You will reach the highest of 'highs' one minute and plummet into the depths of despair and disappointment the next.

The rewards can be significant. You could be driving around in the latest model car, wearing nothing but the best brands, sending your children to private schools, and living the lifestyle of the rich and famous. However, this will not come to you on a platter. It comes with extremely hard work and it depends on the area in which you will be based in, and the median price of the area. You may not be reaching quite those heights in a lower to medium socio-economical area as opposed to if you were a salesperson in the top end of the market selling multi-million-dollar properties which bring huge commissions, but also can bring you bigger problems along with the cash.

For those who are perhaps just coming into the market for the first time, as your first job, my suggestion would be to crawl before you walk. Choose a busy office in a cheaper area. Or if you feel you would feel more comfortable working in a slightly better area, go to the middle of the range in house prices. Often it is not how much you make but how you invest with what you do make.

NEWBIES TO REAL ESTATE - WHAT TO LOOK FOR IN AN OFFICE

As new people to the industry, I have seen many arrive, bright eyed and bushy tailed, excitement turns to fear and within trepidation. Confident and bright, certificate and license in hand are not all you are going to need. My suggestion would be to start in a small friendly office where there is someone to mentor you in your first year (at least) After between 30 – 50 properties sold, you will have possibly covered most 'scenarios' of what happens before, during and after your purchasers go to contract. Only after you have done this, is when you could possible start looking around for a larger office, with a higher profile and bigger Rent Roll as your second bite of the cherry. You would have done your 'apprenticeship' and now more experienced and confident. But remember, it depends on the climate of the industry at the time, in a slow market it could take you 2-4 years to obtain that many contracts.

Having sold this many properties, you would have learned how to deal not only with annoyed Sellers, anxious Buyers, had contracts 'crash' and learned the reasons why, how to pick them up and get them back on track again, but also learned how to deal with dishonest and unscrupulous Sales Agents, your competitors out in the field, but also and unfortunately, within your own office, your own colleagues....yes, unfortunately, the bigger the Dollar $$$ the bigger the SHARK...and they will gobble you up if your inexperienced.

Ask all the right questions. Remember that you are interviewing them. Try not to fall into the trap of losing control of the interview by agreeing with all that is put forward. They are the ones who are looking for someone to fit in with their team, but it is your life, your career, the best thing for you to do is to ask lots of questions. In this eBook you will find a check list of strategic questions to ask., print them out and take it with you to your interview.

If at the very least, you do not feel comfortable in firing a new employer questions at your interview, then ask for his business card and tell him that if you think of anything, he has not covered you will email your queries. When you get back to your computer, send him the list of questions I have incorporated in this book.

Politely ask him if he would mind jotting down some brief answers to the following questions. I am sure you will find that your new employer will think how organised you are and have no problems with responding with all the information you are needing.

If at the interview, poised with pen and paper, the interviewer rushes through the meeting and fobs you off or avoids answering your questions, then should you take on a job with this kind of person, you may find that all through your working days with this man, you will be finding the same thing time and time again particularly when it comes down to Commissions and how it is broken up, you may find it will be a constant battle.

However, on the other hand, if the person interviewing you seems to hang onto your every word, is open and honest with his answers and job descriptions, will put it in writing in an employment agreement, seems hopeful that you are interested in the position, then this could just 'be the one'. If you have all the box's ticked, then it won't be long and you will be in a job you love, making good money and most of all, 'learning the trade'.

Don't give up, this is a fantastic career that you could be proud of. You may not be a Doctor or Psychiatrist, Mathematician, or Vet, but you are a Professional and making more money than they could only dream of making.

THE EXPERIENCED AGENT

This is for you too

If you have been in the industry for some time but feel you can do better for yourself? This is just the perfect book for you to read. I will help you get what you want. Don't be like many agents, going from office to office, interview after interview only to make the same mistakes over and over.

Learn the tools to obtain a better position or renegotiate your present position. As an experienced agent, you already know the possibilities of high earnings, a job that is flexible. A job where you can take time out to pick up the children. Take a family member to a doctor's appointment, grab lunch with a client or old friend. This is a wonderful career if you learn to work Smarter not Harder.

CURIOUS YET?

"But it looks SOOO glamorous!"

Wondering what it would be like to be a real estate agent?

If you are wondering what to do to get into this industry first few steps, this is where to start. I will show you every step you should take. After you read this, you will feel more confident to move forward and take the right steps to start your new chosen career in Real Estate.

Most people have a misconception of what being a real estate agent would be like. They think it looks glamorous, all you have to do all day is show people houses, you get to be in some of the most beautiful homes, entertain a lot and get invited to Seller's parties, etc....

Boy are you in for a rude shock!!! Real estate is darn hard work. You get more knocks than Muhammad

Ali....... Not physically (although that is a possibility in some property arena's) but emotionally and financially. Your ego gets shattered to pieces; you may cry in your car after a Seller has kicked you out their door because you didn't get them the price they wanted, or the settlement date was extended by the buyer and all the Seller's plans, flights, removalists, hotel accommodation, have cost them a pretty penny to have the date moved....and guess what? Yep, it's all YOUR fault. There will be times you will hear the word 'SF'.... yes, a knee-jerk reaction from a disgruntled Buyer or Seller.

Sellers and buyers NEVER take responsibility and solicitors are worse by blaming the other side for 'stuff-ups'....... Hmm.... And you still want to be a real estate agent? Then keep reading, you might just make a good real estate agent if this didn't frighten you.

ALREADY AN EXPERIENCED AGENT?

Still haven't found that right office culture?

You are asking the WRONG questions.

As an experienced Real Estate Sales Consultant and ultimately Company owner, I can assure you I have had my share of interviews and jumping ship only to find myself either in the same situation or even a worse one.

Year after year, still loving the industry, but hating to walk back through the door in the mornings, going home at night only to be wishing I didn't have to return the next day, month after month, year after year until it just got too much.

What was I doing wrong? How come I kept making the same mistakes every time?

The interviews were fine, I held my own in an aggressive industry, confident I would get the job, ... And I always did. But it always turned out to be a different thing altogether once I had been at the new office a week, (sometimes it would take longer, and for those Rookies who are reading this, you might ask "How come it took you that long to realise you had chosen a 'dud' office?")

Those experienced agents reading this, will know exactly where I am going with this. Right? Rookies... take note, if you want to find a great office culture that is fair and honest right from the Principal down to the admin girl, you need to read this over and over again. This is your 'Bible' of working as a real estate agent.

JUMPING SHIP... AGAIN... AND... AGAIN...

I would realise that I had made a huge mistake, but already had some listings, earned the trust of both Vendors and Buyers and yet, all I wanted to do was jump ship.

Once you have started to roll, it is very hard to pull away.... **extremely** hard. Experienced agents know exactly what I am talking about. The longer you stay, the more leads you get, the higher your profile becomes within the area and so on, hence, the harder to leave.

RESIGNING WILL RUIN YOUR CAREER

LEAVING AN OFFICE WILL SET YOU BACK SIX MONTHS – DETRIMENTAL TO YOUR CAREER

To leave the office you're in and start all over again in another area is detrimental to your career, (that is of course, if you are serious about a career in Real

Estate) it sets you back to a point that sometimes you might never gain that back.

This is fact, happened to me personally and to other very good, high profile agents I know, so I know what I am talking about.

This is why you must ask the right questions at your interview, both Rookie and Experienced.

STAY IN THE SAME AREA

DON'T MOVE OUT OF YOUR ZONE

If you absolutely must leave that office, don't run away

with your tails between your legs like I did!!!! Seriously! Stay within the same area that you have been marketing yourself. People already have your magnets on their fridges and recognise you and your car. They know who to call when they want to sell. PLEASE

STAY IN THAT AREA.

ONE LIFE TO LIVE

Time is of the essence

This is the reason I have written this book. ALL AGENTS young and mature, rookie and experienced.... This book is so very important to you all, me included.

We only have one life. While we are young, we can hang around a little while until something "comes along" but we are in no hurry. Right?

However, for those more **mature agents** who don't have that privilege, time is of the essence. You cannot waste time waiting for something else to "come along", you must take the bull by the horns and get cracking.

YOUR INTERVIEWS

There are 10 main questions that you should ask at your interview. If you do not ask these questions, you will be chasing your tail for that 'perfect' position that will NEVER come. These questions will give you the answers (one hopes) that will help your decision in accepting the position when and if you are offered it.

PREPARATION

But before we let you know what these 6 questions are, let's first prepare you for the interview first. I once applied online for a position through an employment agency. Most of the requirements were straight forward.

- Bring along any Licenses, tickets, References, proof of Awards, Superannuation details in case you accept the job on the spot.
- Driver's License
- **Please dress as if you are going to an interview.**

Hulloooo???? AS IF you are going to an interview??? I found this humorous and curious. Surely you would dress no other way but in your very best to impress??

Are you serious?? And yet, time and time again, we read it in the job descriptions on recruitment websites. One has to wonder how some people actually turn up for their interview dressed like a 'dog's breakfast'.

UNTIL I got there, sitting in a room full of interviewees! Looking around, I could see the reason why the employment agency asked for this. There were people there in clothes that I would not wear to the supermarket let alone an interview. Some did not even bother to shave.

One lady had chipped nail polish, uneven nails, some chewed, open toe shoes, leg that had not seen a razor blade in months......, you would think that she would've found a pair that hid her dirty feet! AND chewing gum. Another guy had a nice shirt on but had stubbies and deck shoes??? OMG No wonder I got the job!

Why might I ask do employers and recruitment agencies feel they have to ask us to wear something decent to our interview? Is it not common sense to dress up and try to impress? Do we not "Want" the job?

WHAT NOT TO WEAR – TO BE SUCCESSFUL

How many times have you arranged to meet someone and when they turn up, all you can think is "???" Well, this is exactly what your clients will think of you when you arrive on their doorstep dressed like a 16-year-old heading to a party., or off to the beach after you list their beautiful home.

Your most important 'Asset' is your appearance. Business - like…. Business - like…… business - like…… NOTHING LESS.

5 THINGS NOT TO WEAR AT AN APPOINTMENT

Ladies:

- Mini Skirt
- Plunging neckline
- Strong Perfume

- Chewed or extra-long fingernails
- Extra high heels and platforms

Men:

- Heavy colognes
- Open neck shirts exposing jewellery and chest hair.
- Shorts
- Sandals
- Denim and Leather
- Mullets - Pigtails – Beards GO!!!

Guys leave the jewellery at home; you don't want to look like 'Mr T'…. If a tie is not a requirement, make sure your shirt is buttoned up almost to the last button.

Always carry a jacket (not leather) in your car. You will win the listing over other agents if you are dressed professionally. That does not mean wearing any of the above. Wear a suit, if you don't have a dress jacket, at least wear a collar and tie, dress shoes and a soft cologne.

It never ceased to amaze me when I went to Real Estate Conventions in the City. I was absolutely blown away at the attire of many of the agents there. Some even looked as if they had pulled out a shirt from the clothes basket, crushed and ugly. The casual gear that was neither office wear nor beach wear, but somewhere in between. ... and yes, this seemed to be their working 'style'. It all seemed so unprofessional.

The essence of being business like is to not wear any on the list below. If the client is a husband and wife, you will not win the listing if your boobs are in her husband's face. Be a lady at all times, focus on how you dress and act at all times.

REMEMBER THIS

PREPARE FOR YOUR INTERVIEW

- Take notes from this book. Write down in order the questions you want to ask. Leave half a page per question for the answers as they are given. Don't be afraid to ask for a moment to jot down a few points, or to ask them to repeat something you think you missed. He/she will be impressed. Questioning techniques and taking of notes is a skill learned by successful salespeople.

- GET IT IN WRITING!!!!!!! Do NOT walk out that door until you have received in your little red-hot hand, your Employment Agreement or Contract. Read it carefully and get someone who you feel has the 'nouse' to pick up any mistakes... or should I say... 'Cons' fine print that will affect your ability to earn an above average income in it. Be sure it is a fair 'playing field' for all. Ask for the next couple of days to read the contract before signing.

Be tough, take control of the interview, remember that you are interviewing <u>them</u>.

Ask these important questions, if you don't and get the job,... you will regret it later.

DON'T BE A DREAMER
Take *Control* *of your* *Interview*

YOUR GETTING BIG BUCKS

SHOW RESPECT

- Don't miss that listing.

The client is paying you excellent money to sell their home, in some cases you will receive tens of thousands at the top end of the market, just on the sale of one home and you have the gaul to dress shabbily?? Get real. If you have no understanding of style and some don't, most large department stores and some smaller boutiques for both men and women have 'Style Co-ordinators' that you can book. They will make you look a million dollars. It will come with a cost of course, but worth every dollar.

Don't forget your crowning glory! Yes, your hair! Men, if you have a plate, I will sincerely suggest you get rid of it. If, however your hairstyle reflects your religion or culture, perhaps it be best to find an office in an area that would be more accepting of this otherwise you will be forever explaining away your style.

There is nothing nicer that a neat, modern hairstyle for both men and woman. Take regular visits to your local hairdresser, remember too that you should always be 'networking' and what better way than to talk the ear off the hairdresser, talk real estate, ask them if they own their home, do they know anyone who is thinking of selling, you have a captive audience right with you for an hour or so. Go get em!!

Okay, so now we have 'Dressed you', 'Educated you', 'Scolded you', 'Insulted you!'.........

It is now time to teach you the 10 Mistakes to avoid at your next interview. The 10 questions you should ask to prevent you making another wrong decision by choice of office to work in.

10 STRATEGIC QUESTIONS TO ASK

1. Are you a Selling Principal?

2. Do you have a Rent Roll?

3. How many Rental Properties do you have?

4. Do you have Farming areas?

5. What area will be my Farm?

6. What are the rules of the Farming areas?

7. Do you have a Roster?

8. What are the rules for the Roster?

9. What is my Rate of Commission?

10. Do you offer a Retainer –

Do I have to pay it back?

THE REASONS WHY YOU ASK

10+ ANSWERS

Q1 ARE YOU A SELLING PRINCIPAL?

This is the most important question you need to ask; it is at the top of your list.

Do NOT feel embarrassed to ask this question and leave regretting it. This is one of the 2 main questions to ask as per Sales training in Real Estate.

I personally have been in offices where the boss also is a salesperson. This is thwart with danger!! The last thing you need is to have a sales colleague as a boss as well. But the worst thing that can happen here is this.

The Boss pays the wages and overheads. This can mount to tens of thousands every month and must be paid on time. Yes! Seriously! Tens of thousands!

So, what happens when an enquiry comes into the office? Nine out of ten times, the receptionist is wanting to please the boss and puts the enquiry through to him/her. Suddenly, there is a lovely new listing entered onto the sales board with their name. A listing that, if they sell it, they get 100% of the commission which, depending on the calibre of the property, could be anywhere from a few thousand to tens of thousands, even in the vicinity of a 6-figure commission!!! Particularly if you are selling within an affluent area and you miss out!

ASK YOURSELF:

"HOW WOULD I FEEL IF MY PRINCIPAL WAS THE TOP LISTER AND SELLER OF THE MONTH?"

If you are in a Selling Principal office, get out now.

I can tell you now that I have been in such an office, where the principal reached the top salesperson, and top lister of the month combined in not only their own office but also within their Brand combined, reaching the status of the 'State's Top Salesperson', and you can only guess why!

At the sales meetings each week the principal holds the floor. Each salesperson is asked what they have achieved in the last week and what they have planned for the following week. When it comes around to them, they are so very proud to spruse off to the group (their competitors and colleagues) how wonderfully they have done and that you should follow their lead. Humm……yep, they have truly lost their way. They have forgotten what it was like before they owned the business. They have become greedy to say the least.

I have been in a position where I was not in the office when one of my Developers came to see me and list a large block of land. The commission alone would have been a 6-figure payout. When he arrived, the receptionist called out the Boss who was also an owner. This particular boss said that I was away on holidays and that she would list the property on my behalf. Hence, the property was listed in her name, plus she already had buyers on the back burner **looking for such properties and before I entered the office, she had a contract on the property. She got 100% of the sales commission, again a 6-figure amount. I walked. Never looked back.**

So, you not only have the other sales personnel to compete with, you more often than not, have the

Principal (your boss) listing and selling against you as well.

** Another situation to warn you about is the Boss who says this:

"No, I have given sales up. Only when an old friend or old client from the past that wants only me to sell their property do I list" ….

Yeh right!!!!!!DO NOT believe this. It's a common line a Selling Principal uses just to soften the blow. They have been in the industry probably since before you left high school. Can you imagine how many clients they have served since then? Yes, they would be very busy indeed.

This is a Red Flag!! Do not accept a job in this office.

What he is really saying is "Yes, I list and sell anything that I want, I am the boss and whatever leads come in, I get to see them first, if I like what I see I will list them, If I don't, I will let it go to the person on Rosters! The salespeople will get the 'crumbs. If you hear this…" Thank you, nice meeting you" and walk never look back. This office is not for you.

If you want to be successful, this is not the way to choose an office, you will never be as successful as your Boss who is stealing all the top-quality listings and selling them before you can call up your buyers on your own data base.

Q2 DO YOU HAVE A RENT ROLL?

There are 2 main questions that trainers for the Real Estate License discuss and warn you about when in search of an office to work in. The question we have just discussed and this one.

If you look at the size of the staff in a real estate agency, Salesperson, Reception, Administration, Property Management and in some offices, they have a Marketing Manager. If you look at what the average wage is in today's times, you will see that the overheads for a Real Estate office are huge indeed.

When the Sales market slides, and this is often caught unawares, all of the above still have to be paid. Where do they get their money to keep the doors open when they might be lucky to only sell a house or two a month in bad times?

THE RENT-ROLL PAYS THE BILL. Without the rent-roll, you won't be offered a RETAINER and get lower commission rates.

Q3 HOW MANY RENTAL PROPERTIES IN YOUR PORTFOLIO

THE RENT ROLL …. its GOLD…. to YOU

The bigger the Rent Roll, the bigger the income from it. Anywhere up to 12% in some countries is the going rate, on the weekly rental.

VIP This is a very important thing to remember.

It is well known that on an average, 10% of a rent roll (property management portfolio) – or in layman's

terms, 'homes and units rented out' on their books) will be placed on the market for sale. Investors have various reasons to sell their investment property. Perhaps their Accountant at the end of the financial year has advised them to either 'off load' some capital or go out and purchase another investment property.

So, if there are 100 rental properties, each year approximately 10 of these properties come back onto the market for sale and most times are listed at the office that holds the Rental. This sounds like a lot of rentals. But if there is a team of say 6 or 7 (or more) salespeople, you may be lucky to get 'one' of those listings.

** If the office has 1,000+ rentals on their books (and in some areas this is not unheard of, I know of one office that has been in business for more than 30 years, business just keeps rolling through the doors) 10% of this is 100 listings that will filter down through to the Sales Agents thought the year. But 10% of 10,000 listings? Needless to say, it is a family business and several of the salespeople are family members, but who cares, if it is run with integrity you each agent will be making an above average income.

This is on top of the listings you will get from what walks in the door on your roster and old clients that are wanting to resell with you. THIS is why it is a question you must ask at your interview!!

You do the figures!!

Q4 DO YOU HAVE FARMNG AREAS?

What are Farming Areas you may ask??

Your boss may tell you that they don't have Farming Areas. This is ok for the experienced agent with a huge data base of clients from the years of selling. But for a newbie, it is important that you at least choose a patch to call your own.

This is your 'Patch' in which you will be working in to raise your profile, this will be by way of Letter Box drops, Phone canvassing, attending council meetings for updates on the area, networking, setting up stalls at the schools within or close to your Farming area, and much more.

BE THE EXPERT IN YOUR AREA

The farming area given to you, may be of up to 3,000 homes or more or less. It is your own responsibility to get to know your area and what it has going for it so that when a seller calls you, you can be seen to be up to date on all development and happenings in the area.

This will please your seller and help obtain the listing.

Q5 WHAT AREA WILL BE MY FARM?

Farming areas ONLY WORK if strict office rules are in place and maintained closely.

EXAMPLE: You could be doing the hard slog, letter box dropping, climbing hills in the middle of Summer or Winter, having dogs snap at your heels only to get back to the office and find that one of the people you have just dropped a flyer in their box has called the office number on the flyer before you could get back and the call has been put through to another sales person who now has the listing!!

This is YOUR INCOME. Never forget this. If this happens to you, you have lost thousands of dollars from a letter box drop because the office receptionist did not get trained to ask the right questions to the caller.

WHERE IS THE LINE DRAWN?

Your farming area is more than likely going to back up against the farming area of another agent. This can be tricky, find out the 'clear line' between both farms or there will be 'blood'.

Q6 WHAT ARE THE RULES OF THE FARMING AREAS?

When you ask the interviewer about Farming areas, don't forget to ask how it works in this office. If their rules do not suit you, don't bother with the next few questions. No matter how knowledgeable you sound, the boss will only see you as a troublemaker and you won't get the job anyway.

- If you've just letterbox dropped and an enquiry comes in off your brochure, and another agent gets a listing from your hard work? How is this dealt with by management? What are the rules here?

** Another rule of thumb, in the next category we will cover Rosters. Rosters and Farming areas often go hand in hand. But without Farming areas you still need a Roster to prevent favouritism from the Boss and the Receptionists etc.

Q7 DO YOU HAVE A ROSTER SYSTEM

This is an important point particularly if there are Farming Area but still important nonetheless in your office as mentioned in the previous category 'Farming Areas'.

At your interview, ask the following questions:

1. If it is my roster time, and I get an enquiry to appraise someone's property, if I am on Roster, what is office procedure?
2. While I am away, and I am on Roster, can the receptionist take enquiries for me for when I return or does the enquiry go straight to the next rostered agent?
3. If a buyer walks in right on the boarder of my roster finishing and another one starting, who gets the client?
4. If I have been letter box dropping and networking in my farming area, but an enquiry comes through from my hard work, does it come directly to me or does the other sales consultant on Roster get the enquiry, hence the listing or sale? Yes, we did cover this, but this is such an important issue.

5. What if I am on the phone talking to a client and there is another enquiry coming through? Does the receptionist say I will get back to them when I get off the phone or is it put through to someone else?

Q8 WHAT ARE YOUR RULES FOR THE ROSTER SYSTEM?

Although Farming areas and Rosters are common in this industry, not all offices have them. In fact, I have worked really well doing my own thing in an office that gave free reign, I could list and sell anywhere and was not bound to the office on a Roster System. It can of course bring problems with competitive sales agents, or whingers, but if you try to work a little out of your area, there will be less competition from salespeople in your own office.

This is a highly paid industry, and the higher the commission on high end properties, the more aggressive the sales consultants can become. Unless there are some very strict rules of behaviour, the competitive nature in us all raises its ugly head.

ARGUMENTS & FIGHTS

Don't be surprised to witness heated arguments and fisty cuffs happen in your office. This too is most common. I personally have experienced the wrath of another agent in my own office, getting shoved against a wall, had other agents 'steal' enquiries, fossick through your desk and diary. Many a salesperson has been known to give 'kick backs' to

Rental Property managers, when an investor decides he wants to sell his rental property, he calls his property manager and asks her to assist in having the sales team list and sell it. If there is no ROSTER or strict OFFICE RULES, there are opportunities there for kickbacks to take place. This is unfair and dishonest but good to know so that you can ask the appropriate questions at your next interview.

I know of one Principal who has been in the industry many years, he has a security monitor on his office and security cameras in the Sales Room, overlooking all the Salespeople's desks. If any salesperson goes to another's desk without permission, they are instantly dismissed. The principal will walk up to that salesperson, tap them on the shoulder and tell them to leave, stands there as they clear out their desk and escorts them to the door., never to return again.

Wow, he is my hero!!!

That is a principal who knows the nature of the beast in this industry.

Q9 COMMISSIONS – WHAT RATE COMMISSION?

In countries around the world, commission rates and agents wage or retainers differ immensely. So, you are going to have to do your own homework on this for your State/Country/County.

So, what figures you will see in this chapter, are only based on my own area and industry regulations.

However, based on what I write, and the breakdowns, you will get the 'gist' of it for your own areas based on your country's or states regulations, and it will give you an idea of what to ask.

Don't forget to find out what the regulated commissions are in your area first. Do your homework, don't look silly to your interviewer by asking a ridiculous question.

You will need to ask the following questions. Don't be shy, the questions in this Brief book may seem a little intimidating to ask but believe me when I say that your interviewer will be 'expecting' you to ask them.

Q10 WHAT IS YOUR OFFICE POLICY ON 'COMMISSION BREAK-UP'?

Commission Breakup

You would be extremely lucky to get as much as 50% commission in your first year. Extremely lucky indeed. In fact, you could very well only get as little as 35%.

Some offices say that you get to list and sell your own listings, so you get 100% of the commission. But remember this is not 100% of the 'whole' commission. It is 100% of Sales Consultants commission which could be the agreed amount in your employment agreement such as for example 100% of the agreed 35% Sales Consultant's commission.

Large franchise brands want their royalties. So instead of the 10% coming off the top of all takings, they first hit you the salesperson up for a 10% franchise fee. So, your commission first of all is reduced by 10% Fair? No, but it happens, and you really must read your contract and have a friend go over it for you too.

If it is in an office where you can all sell the listings regardless of who lists it in the first place, then you list the property and the other salesperson sells the property, the Lister may get slightly more commission than the seller. Or it may be equally divided up.

For example: A Salesperson's commission percentages and breakups.

> 35% +65% = 100% (35% to the Sales People - 65% to the Office)
>
> So, when you (the lister) owns a listing and the other sales person has the buyer, he sells the property, the commission is broken up. The amount of commission disbursed depends on the office 'Commission Structure and Break-up. Usually the Lister gets a higher rate of commission than the Seller.
>
> This could be 60/40%,... 30/70%,... 35/65%.....but remember that this is only of the Sales Persons portion of the commission, the office still gets a good hunk of it as mentioned.
>
> Breakup – So lets say that another sales person sells your new listing? If the office sales commission break up, keeping it simple for this book only, it is 50/50 and this is only of the sales people commission.
>
> You - half of 50% = 25% (25% of 100% of the full commission)
>
> Other Sales person - half of 50% = 25% (25% of 100% of the full commission)

Some offices may offer more as mentioned to the Lister, because without the listing there would be no funds at all. There is some office that will pay as high as 70/80%. There is often a catch to this, you may not get a retainer at this level or you may be classed as a contractor. Question thoroughly any kind of offer such as this.

So there for the breakup may be still 35% to the sales team. Then the Lister will get 60% and the Seller will get 40% but this is not of the full office 100%, it is of the 35% remember?

Now take out your calculator and do yourself up some figures. Work out how much over a year you could make based on a full 35% per Sale.

Often commissions can be negotiated at the meeting. Your principal may offer you a certain percentage, and if this does not suit you can come back with a counter percentage.

However, do not be seen to be greedy because in my way of thinking, when you are learning, half a loaf of bread is better than none. You can always renegotiate your percentages down the track after you have proven your sales ability with figures you have done in the first 12 months.

If you fly blind, do not ask about the commission structure at your interview, and only find out when your employment agreement/contract is drawn up, it is too late to negotiate, and you will have to prove yourself over the next 12 months before obtaining a higher rate.

Don't think you Rookies are the only ones who do this, Experienced Agents also get caught up in the moment at the interview trying to impress the Boss with their personality only to walk out kicking themselves because they didn't raise this subject.

Q11 DO YOU OFFER A RETAINER/WAGE?

WHAT ARE THE CONDITIONS OF THE RETAINER?

- Do you pay a retainer? If so, how much is it?
- Do I have to pay the retainer back?
- If I do, then do they come out of my commissions all at once?
- What is the commission percentage you pay? 70% 50% 30% or other?
- Don't forget that when they tell you., ask is that 70% of 100% of the full commission – This is very important a question as you will see later in this book.
- When do I get the commission paid? As soon as the Property Settles. Straight away or is there a delay of 7 days, 14 days or more, and why?
- What comes out of my commission, Tax, social club, Printing and advertising costs? Anything else?
- What is the breakdown with conjunctions?

RETAINER OR BASE WAGE

This is sometimes a weekly retainer which then comes off your first commission. However, in some offices, due to the marketing of yourself and of the office, your employer may offer a regular 'wage' rather than a retainer but give less on the Commission. There was a time that Real Estate Sales teams were working on a Commission only basis, however now by law in most states, the Agencies must pay a to new agents coming into the industry in most countries and it must be of a legal rate.

CHECK WITH YOUR 'FAIR WORK' or GOVERNMENT

Don't rely on what a principal will tell you that you are entitled to, contact your State's Government departments, or Fair Work on Wages and Commissions. Labour and Industries do your research. My best friend is 'Google'.

YOU MUST ASK THIS QUESTION – DON'T BE FOOLED RETAINERS

You MUST ask questions about your retainer and how, and if, it has to be paid back. Don't be foolish thinking you can trust this person to do the right thing. Real estate offices have huge overheads and if there is a way, they can use your commission to get them over the months bills they will do it.

Having to pay it back can pose a stressful situation for you in a slow market. You could work for 3 months while marketing your profile before actually getting a Listing let alone a sale. This of course means that you have accumulated some approximate debt of $9-$10,000 so your first couple of sales are eaten up by your retainers. As mentioned, do your homework and find out the regulations in your area.

However, you may be as lucky as I was. I started my first day in a Booming market. Within a week I had my first listing and sold it by the end of the month, with several more in that month, so I was only in the Red for a couple of weeks, retainer paid back in full and a few thousand in the bank. I never looked back. But it could have been far different.

It could be argued whether in fact you actually do have to repay a retainer. In the court of law, it may well be that the judge will see you as a 'Victim', While you are receiving a retainer, you are out in the public pounding the pavement, knocking on doors, letter box dropping, networking, and all the time promoting the boss's company. His real estate Brand is on all the brochures, business cards you are handing out, every phone call you are making you are singing their praises.

"Good morning Mrs Jones, this is Mary-Lou from Smith's Realty" ....

So, Smith's Realty is getting plugged on a daily basis by an agent who is getting paid a retainer. In my opinion, this is no different to paying a marketing team, or their office manager a wage. So why do they think that they can take the money back that they call a retainer if you wish to leave their employ?

So, don't stress about having to "Pay back the retainer". It might pay you to speak to a solicitor before signing on the dotted line.

DO NOT ACCEPT A POSITION THAT IS COMMISSION ONLY

This is not directed at the experienced long-term agent. It's for the newbies.

One state in Australia recently improved things for the new salespeople entering the industry. Principals MUST pay a weekly wage with all the fringe benefits along with it such as Superannuation etc. Plus, commission which is negotiable. It can be a sliding scale wage against commission. However not all states or countries have changed the rules and still it is commission only.

This is the fastest way to go broke for you newbies, you may lose your home and even your spouse due to the enormous strain it will have on your relationship and finances. No matter how great the interviewer is at telling you that you will have your first listing in a day or two and sale by the end of the month.... this is 'pie in the sky' crap. If you believe in this, you probably believe in the tooth fairy. Trust me, as a real estate agent who has jumped from office to office in search of that illusive perfect job, I know what I am talking about when I tell you that it is quite rare to have your first listing and sale in the first month "unless' you have entered at the perfect time. Yes, and I did this as you will see in this eBook. But there were other offices also that took me literally months to get my first sale.

IMPORTANT POINTS TO REMEMBER

TO OBTAIN A HIGH INCOME AND BECOME A HIGHLY RESPECTED AGENT IN YOUR AREA

The Lister:

A successful Lister of property, maybe it lands, apartments, penthouses or just residential, are highly respected by any employer. If you are a top lister, your sales team will love you because not all sales agents can close that deal. They can sell but can't get that listing. So, the Lister in an office is worth their weight in cold.

Keep listing. Don't look back. List.... list...list. This will bring you a high income eventually. You can go on holiday and still make money. The Sales Team will be endeavouring to sell all your listings. As you sip on your cocktail on the deck of a cruise ship or yacht, sailing Europe, your counterparts are slogging it hard signing contracts on your 'listings'. Woo hoo! Your beauty!!

However, do not lose sight of your job description. You must also stay in touch with your sellers if only by email or skype while you're on the high seas. In my next book you will find out why this is so important for the future of a successful real estate agent.

IT'S HARD WORK

Agents beware

Remember that success comes at a cost. To be a successful real estate agent you must be focused. Your social life and family commitments will suffer, there will be late nights and early mornings, weekend work, you could work for 2 weeks without a day off. You could burn out. There will be lean times as well because a buoyant market has got to slow down and eventually could actually stop for months at a time, depending on the world economy, your local industry etc. So be prepared, in the good times, don't go out and buy homes you may not be able to afford when the market dips. Or flashy cars that have their own mortgage plus payments on their partner's car, house mortgage etc.

FINANCIAL SUICIDE

This is financial suicide. I have seen agents take on the appearance of being very successful and wealthy only to see their cars in sales yards, on street corners with For Sale signs on them and their homes placed on the market when the industry slides and they can no longer sustain the payments. This can destroy any strong and successful agent's self-esteem and self-worth, not to mention their relationships. Confidence shattering to say the least. Don't let this be you. Do not live "in the moment".

PRACTICE YOUR SPEEL

YOUR MIRROR IS A GREAT TOOL

Read this book over and over, memorise the questions and a perfect too is your own bedroom or bathroom mirror.

When no one is at home, take your list to the mirror and pretend you are being interviewed by the person in the mirror.

Do this as many times as it takes for you to retain the questions you are going to ask and how to ask them. Use your own words or it will sound false and rehearsed.

When you get the job, it is also a great way to practice your spiel you're going to use with your clients when you are listing or selling.

REMEMBER THIS

PREPARE FOR YOUR INTERVIEW

Take notes from this book. Write down in order the questions you want to ask. Leave half a page per question for the answers as they are given. Don't be afraid to ask for a moment to jot down a few points, or to ask them to repeat something you think you missed. He/she will be impressed. Questioning techniques and taking of notes is a skill learned by successful salespeople.

GET IT IN WRITING!!!!!!! Do NOT walk out that door until you have received in your little red-hot hand, your Employment Agreement or Contract. Read it carefully and get someone who you feel has the 'nouse' to pick up any mistakes... or should I say... 'Cons' fine print that will affect your ability to earn an above averageincome in it. Be sure it is a fair 'playing field' for all.

Ask for the next couple of days to read the contract before signing.

FUNNIES - Beware those 'Lil White Lies'

Copyright – Sue Edman-Beckenham

FUNNIES- You didn't know about the millionTermites?

Copyright – Sue Edman-Beckenham

A FINAL WARNING

Please remember that when working as a Realtor, you are running your own business within a business. You only get out of it what you put into it.

I am no expert, just a realtor who has done the hard yard for you to benefit from my advice.

I have seen so many great agents leave the industry due to bad choices they made from day 1.

Remember the Basics on what to watch out for are here.

- Don't choose an office with a Selling Principal.
- Know the right questions to ask at your interview.
- Have someone check your Employment Agreement before signing it.
- If a Newbie, don't try working from home. You won't learn anything. You need to be in an office.
- Read all the Questions & Answers in this book thoroughly.
- Read internet Reviews on the company.

- Choose an office that has a high profile, one that is selling the most in your chosen area.
- Make sure they have a large Rent Roll; this will bring you sales off it.

EAT – BREATH – SLEEP REAL ESTATE

If you go into this industry expecting it to be easy, and that the sellers and buyers will walk in the door on your roster, then you are mistaken.

Nothing will land in your lap. You have to work hard for your money, early mornings, late evenings, weekends and interruptions at family events.

*

- Never turn off your phone no matter what the occasion. Put it on silent if you must at Weddings and funerals.
- Check your emails hourly!
- Never knock back a showing
- Don't be late to appointments!
- Remember who is paying your commission. Is it the Seller or the Buyer? Are you a Sellers Agent or a Buyers Agent? Be loyal. Remember

"Loose Lips – Sink Ships"

ALWAYS BE HONEST

Eat, Breath, Sleep

REAL ESTATE ©

A NOTE FROM THE WRITER

Marely a retired realtor.

Congratulations on deciding to enter the real estate industry. It is an industry that offers it's sales people

Flexability – Self Worth – Confidence – New friends – An excellent Income – Wealth & Opportunities.

Never give up trying, never let down your clients and always be honest, hold yourself high with integrity, and it will serve you well.

I love it and so will you.

Good luck!

Your caring realtor

Sue Edman-Beckenham

ANOTHER BIG THANKS

To all the Sellers and Buyers, thank you for your business and being great clients. It has been a wonderful journey; I have met some wonderful people.

I've had some great colleagues and boss's; I hope you Newbies are as lucky as I have been. Thanks for all the Laughs, Conjunctions, Caravans (a real estate term for Stock Runs) I have walked away with some best friends...... You all know who you are! Love you heaps.

THANKS TO REAL ESTATE – HOW WE LOVE TO HATE YOU

You have taught me patience, how to laugh at myself, the art of giving, the art of appreciating everything around me. You have given me the greatest joy any job could offer a person in any industry dealing with the public. You have given me flexibility in my job, the opportunity to meet wonderful people and the strength to stand up for myself, to be strong in the face of one of the most competitive jobs in the world.

"Thank you, Real Estate, you have served me well".

Made in the USA
Columbia, SC
13 September 2022

67136331R00063